Contents

How to use this book

Each page has a title telling you what it is about.

Instructions look like this. Always read these carefully before starting.

This shows you how to set out your work. The first question is done for you.

This is Owl. Ask your teacher if you need to do his questions.

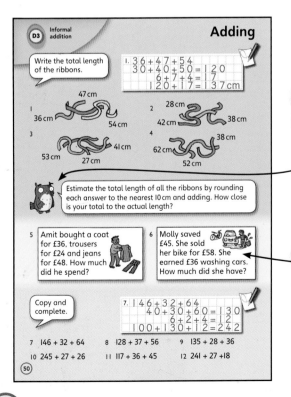

Read these word problems very carefully. Decide how you will work out the answers.

Rounding to the nearest 10

Round each number to the nearest 10.
Use the number line to help.

1. 6 4 → 6 0

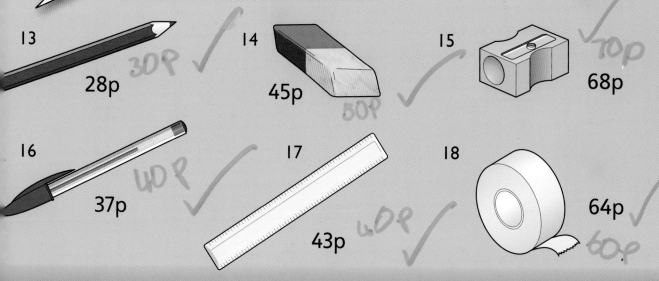

1	64 → 60	2	72 → 70	3	81 → 80	4	46
5	49 → 50	6	53 → 50	7	77 → 80	8	84 → 80
9	75 → 80	10	45 → 50	11	56 → 60	12	61 → 60

Round each price to the nearest 10p.

13. 2 8 p → 3 0 p

13
28p 30p ✓

14
45p 50p ✓

15
68p 70p ✓

16
37p 40p ✓

17
43p 40p ✓

18
64p 60p ✓

Write the numbers that round to 100 as the nearest 10. Write those that round to 200.

Nearest 10, nearest 100

Round each amount to the nearest £100.

1
£125
100 ✓

2
£248
£200 ✓

3
£569
£600 ✓

4
£750
£800 ✓

5
£933
£900 ✓

6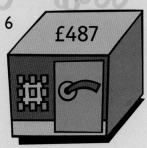
£487
£500 ✓

7
£275
£300 ✓

8
£360
£400 ✓

 Each hedgehog weighs 500 g rounded to the nearest 100 g. If there is a difference of 50 g in their weights, what could each weight be?

Round each number to the nearest 10.

9. 468 → 470

9 468 *470* ✓

10 217 *220* ✓

11 652 *650* ✓

12 712 *710* ✓

13 902 *900* ✓

14 395 *400* ✓

15 555 *560* ✓

16 313 *310* ✓

Nearest 10, nearest 100

Round each price to the nearest 10p. Add the rounded prices. Write the approximate total in pounds and pence.

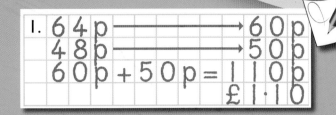

```
1. 64p ────────→ 60p
   48p ────────→ 50p
   60p + 50p = 110p
                £1.10
```

1

64p   48p

40 ✓

2

57p   34p

90,90 ✓

3

78p   27p

80 + 30 = 110

Find the total of all six stamps and round it to the nearest 10p. Find the total of the rounded prices. Are they the same?   *310p   £3.10*

4 Jess owes her mum some money. She has to pay an amount that rounds to £10 to the nearest pound. What is the least she can pay?   *£9*

5 When recording a tape, Mena rounds to the nearest 10 minutes. Her programme is 38 minutes long. What length tape will she need?   *40 mins*

Round to the nearest 10 and the nearest 100.

```
6. 348 → 350
   348 → 300
```

6 348 *350 300*   7 212 *210 200*   8 641 *640 600*   9 772 *770 800*

10 453 *450 500*   11 584 *580 600*   12 633 *630 600*   13 536 *540 100*

Nearest 10p, nearest £1

Round each price to the nearest 10p.

I. £2·43 → £2·40

1  £2·43

2  £4·83

3  £3·35

4  £4·51

5 £6·22

6  £3·95

7  £7·18

8  £6·90

Round each amount to the nearest pound.

9. £4·40 → £4

9  £4·40

10  £3·15

11  £6·60

12 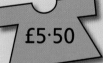 £5·50

13  £8·88

14  £6·06

15 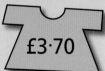 £3·70

16 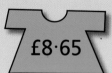 £8·65

17  £7·70

 Estimate how much it would cost to buy all the t-shirts. Add the rounded amounts. How close was your estimate?

Adding and subtracting

Copy and complete.

1. £3·60 + 40p = £4

1 £3·60 + ☐ = £4

2 £2·80 + ☐ = £3

3 £6·50 + ☐ = £7

4 £1·10 + ☐ = £2

5 £3·40 + ☐ = £4

6 £5·70 + ☐ = £6

Each person buys some fruit. Write their change.

7. £4·80 + 20p = £5

7  £4·80 £5

8  £3·60 £4

9  £6·60 £7

10 £3·20 £4

11 £7·50 £8

12 £5·70 £6

How many pairs of amounts from £1 to £3 have a difference of 50p? Both amounts must be multiples of 10p.

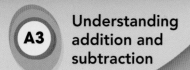
Adding and subtracting

Rewrite as subtractions.

1. £2 − £1·30 = 70p

1 £1·30 + 🍎 = £2

2 £2·70 + 🍊 = £3

3 £1·90 + 🫐 = £2

4 £3·20 + 🍍 = £4

5 £2·40 + 🍎 = £3

6 £4·60 + 🥚 = £5

Copy and complete.

7. £6 − £5·40 = 60p

7 £6 − £5·40

8 £5 − £4·20

9 £10 − £9·30

10 £8 − £7·80

11 £7 − £6·50

12 £5 − £4·10

13 £6 − £5·60

14 £8 − £7·20

15

| Ben has £10 and buys a drink for £2·80. How much does he have left? | He meets Su, who has £5. She buys a sandwich for £4·20. How much does she have left? | They put their money together and buy two tickets for £2·20 each. How much is left? |

Write your own story to represent a subtraction of two amounts of money.

Adding and subtracting

Find the difference between the two heights.

1. $100 - 60 = 40\,cm$

1   100 cm   60 cm

2   110 cm   90 cm

3   200 cm   196 cm

4   150 cm   139 cm

5   70 cm   130 cm

6   190 cm   220 cm

Use the facts to help you complete the following:

$340 + 80 = 420$

$570 - 290 = 280$

$1040 - 680 = 360$

$760 + 570 = 1330$

7    $360 + 680 = \boxed{}$

8    $420 - 80 = \boxed{}$

9    $1330 - 570 = \boxed{}$

10    $290 + 280 = \boxed{}$

11    $420 - 340 = \boxed{}$

12    $420 - \boxed{} = 340$

13    $1330 - \boxed{} = 570$

14    $1040 - 360 = \boxed{}$

15    $3400 + 800 = \boxed{}$

Write an addition of two huge numbers! Write three more additions and subtractions like these.

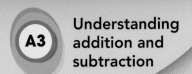
Adding and subtracting

Find the sum.
Find the difference.
Find the difference between these two!

1. £2·20 + £3·50 = £5·70
   £3·50 − £2·20 = £1·30
   £5·70 − £1·30 = £4·40

1

£2·20   £3·50

2

£1·20   £2·60

3

£3·40   £2·20

4

£1·20   £2·50

5

£4·10   £2·70

6

£3·20   £2·40

7

£2·80   £1·10

8

£4·50   £2·30

9

£2·70   £4·10

10

Write two numbers: 7   4
Write the sum: 11
Write the difference: 3
Find the difference between the two: 11 − 3 = 8

Look at this answer and compare it with the original numbers.
Repeat the process. Can you find a pattern?

Adding and subtracting

The stock take in the shop shows how many tins. A delivery arrives. Write the new amount.

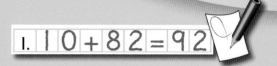

1. $10 + 82 = 92$

1

10 tins

82 tins

2

60 tins

64 tins

3

40 tins

57 tins

4

30 tins

66 tins

5

70 tins

78 tins

6

40 tins

54 tins

Copy and complete.

7. $46 + 70 = 116$

7 $46 + 70 =$

8 $54 + 60 =$

9 $82 + 50 =$

10 $146 + 30 =$

11 $173 + 20 =$

12 $155 + 40 =$

13 $261 + 30 =$

14 $342 + 50 =$

15 $437 + 50 =$

Write your age. If your mum is 20 years older, how old is she? Your gran is 20 years older than her. If this pattern continues, how old is your great great great gran?

11

Adding 2-digit numbers

Add the card numbers.

1. $47 + 36 =$
   $70 + 13 = 83$

1 | 4 0 | 7
     3 0 | 6

2 | 5 0 | 2
       4 0 | 8

3 | 2 0 | 3
       4 0 | q

4 | 7 0 | 8
       1 0 | 7

5 | 6 0 | 3
       4 0 | 8

6 | 3 0 | 6
       2 0 | 7

7 | 5 0 | 3
       6 0 | 6

8 | 4 0 | 5
       7 0 | 4

9 | 3 0 | 3
       5 0 | 7

Add the prices.

10. $48p + 67p = 115p$

10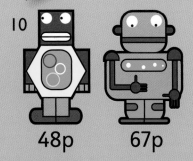
48p   67p

11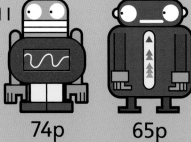
74p   65p

12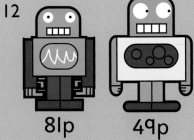
81p   49p

13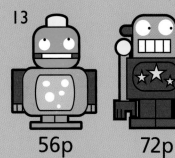
56p   72p

14
47p   63p

15
63p   59p

 Two numbers add to make 121. Each number has both digits the same. What could the numbers be?

Adding 2-digit numbers

How many passengers on the plane now?

I. $68 + 46 = 114$

1 68 passengers
46 get on

2 174 passengers
17 get on

3 152 passengers
28 get on

4 317 passengers
74 get on

5 154 passengers
38 get on

6 128 passengers
63 get on

In what year did each person die?

7. $1837 + 64 = 1901$

7

born 1837

lived for 64 years

8

born 1564

lived for 52 years

9

born 1491

lived for 56 years

10

born 1558

lived for 45 years

11

born 1820

lived for 90 years

12

born 1903

lived for 38 years

Sunil's granny was born in 1924. The year she died had a digit total of 20. How long could she have lived?

Adding 2-digit numbers

Write the number of minutes that must be set on the recorder. Write the time the tape will end.

I. $48 + 37 = 85$ minutes
   $8{:}25$

1
VHS 7:00 REC SP

Westenders: 48 minutes
News update: 37 minutes

2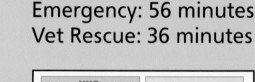
VHS 9:00 REC SP

Emergency: 56 minutes
Vet Rescue: 36 minutes

3
VHS 10:00 REC SP

Coronation Road: 42 minutes
The Magic Seesaw: 39 minutes

4
VHS 8:00 REC SP

Pop Nation: 27 minutes
EuroPop special: 47 minutes

The video tape is 100 minutes long. Which three programmes could you record?

Each child is owed some money. Write the amount they have now.

5. £ 1·64 + 28p = £ 1·92

5
£1·64
owed 28p

6
£1·38
owed 56p

7
£1·29
owed 49p

8
£1·56
owed 37p

9
£1·62
owed 33p

10
£1·42
owed 26p

Doubling

Write the double.

1. double 5 → 10

1  *10*

2  *12*

3  *14*

4  *18*

5  *8*

6  *22*

Double each pile of money.

7. double 30p → 60p

7  *60p*

8 *£1*

9 *£1:20*

10 *80p*

11  *£1:80*

12  *1:60*

13

14  *40p*

15 Chang had 25p pocket money. Her dad doubled it. She spent 10p on a lolly. Her uncle doubled what she had left. How much does she have now?

 Is it better to start with 3p and double it six times or start with 30p and double it twice? Guess first!

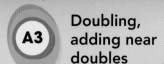

Doubling, adding near doubles

Write the double.

I. double 13 = 26

1  13 double score!

2 17 double score!

3 15 double score!

4  12 double score!

5 14 double score!

6  19 double score!

True or false?

7 Double 19 is more than 10 plus double 9.

8 Double 17 is 2 more than double 16.

9 Double 15 is the same as doubling 5 then doubling the answer.

10 Double 13 is 6 less than double 10.

Copy and complete.

11. double 13 = 26
    13 + 14 = 27

11 13 + 14 =

12 17 + 18 =

13 15 + 16 =

14 12 + 11 =

15 9 + 8 =

16 24 + 25 =

17 19 + 18 =

18 21 + 22 =

 When you add next-door numbers, the answer is always odd. Is this true or false? What if you add numbers with a difference of 2?

Doubling, adding near doubles

Each child's pocket money is doubled. Write the double.

1. double 35p → 70p

1   35p

2 65p

3  85p

4  £1·35

5   70p

6  15p

7  95p

8  25p

9 Tim had 35p. His friend had 1p more. How much did they have together?

10 Sandy is 17 years old. Her friend is 1 year older. How long have they lived in total?

11 Loppy the rabbit weighs 750 g. His sister weighs 10 g more. How much do they weigh together?

Write your own story for 70 + 71.

Complete these additions.

12. double 35 = 70
35 + 36 = 71

12 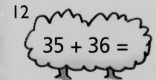 35 + 36 =

13 40 + 41 =

14 25 + 26 =

15 12 + 13 =

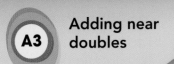
Adding near doubles

Each knight crosses the bridge, rescues the princess and takes her to his tent 10 m away. How far does he go in total?

1. $400 + 410 = 810$ m

10 m   400 m

2
bridge: 350 m

3
bridge: 240 m

4
bridge: 750 m

5
bridge: 600 m

6 Add two numbers. The first is 10 larger than the second. The answer is 510. What are the numbers?

7 Two next-door numbers add to make 3 more than double 24. What are the numbers?

8 Find two next-door numbers which add to make the number 9 less than 100.

9 Add 18 and 19. Add 28 and 29. Add 38 and 39. Can you say the total of 48 and 49 without doing any work?

Take an odd number less than 20. Use two next-door numbers to make it, for example 15 = 7 + 8. Repeat for other numbers. Can you find three next-door numbers which add to make 9, 12, 15 and 18?

Counting in 2s, even and odd

Write the next three numbers in each sequence.

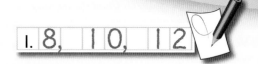
1. 8, 10, 12

1 2, 4, 6...

2 15, 17, 19...

3 41, 43, 45...

4 32, 34, 36...

5 1, 3, 5...

6 14, 16, 18...

Write each number. Identify it as even or odd.

7. 64 even

7 64

8 27

9 31

10 45

11 54

12 18

13 9

14 11

15 Joey had an even number of stickers. When Amit gave him 7 more he had an odd number between 20 and 22. How many did he have?

16 Jade is an even number of years old. She goes to your school. How old could she be?

I have a 2-digit odd number. Both digits add to make an even number less than 10. What could the number be?

Counting in 5s and 50s

The vending machine has some money already. Put in two 5ps. What will the machine show?

 1. 25p 30p

1 20p

2 35p

3 40p

4 80p

5 65p

6 70p

7 50p

8 30p

Write the next three numbers.

9. 350, 400, 450

9 200, 250, 300

10 1000, 1050, 1100

11 600, 650, 700

12 250, 300, 350

13 750, 800, 850

14 400, 450, 500

15 300, 350, 400

16 550, 600, 650

17 700, 750, 800

 How many 50s do we count when counting from 900 to 1900?

Counting in 50s

Count on in 50s three more numbers.

1. 850, 900, 950

1  800

2  600

3  450

4  700

Now count on four numbers.

5  400

6  650

7  300

8  250

True or false? If we are counting on in 50s, starting at 0...

9   ...we do say 650

10   ...we don't say 400

11  ...we do say 615

12   ...we don't say 310

Write each number. Identify it as odd or even.

13. 367 odd

13  367

14 419

15 225

16 404

17 607

18 111

19 912

20 334

 Find this number! It is an even number with 2 digits. The digits add to 9.

Counting

1 Copy and complete the table.

	600	705	750	1005	810	100	48	130	350	950	415
Even/odd	Even										
In 50s count	✓										
In 5s count	✓										

2 When you add the digits of the numbers in the 50s count, you get a pattern. What is the pattern? Start from 50.

250	2 + 5 + 0 = 7
300	3 + 0 + 0 = 3
350	3 + 5 + 0 = 8

Write the next three numbers in the count.

3. 75, 100, 125

3 0, 25, 50

4 150, 175, 200

5 275, 300, 325

6 75, 100, 125

7 50, 75, 100

8 200, 225, 250

9 Sandy has a savings account. Every week she pays in £50. She starts with £300. How many weeks until she has £1000?

10 A water tower leaks 50 l a day. It has 2000 l. How long before it runs dry?

Fours

Copy and complete the grid.

1	2	3	4
5	6		

Write the last number in the:

1 second row   2 tenth row

3 fifth row   4 fourth row

5 third row   6 seventh row

7 sixth row   8 ninth row

Each animal has four legs. Write the number of legs in each set of animals.

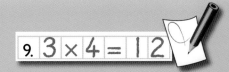

9. $3 \times 4 = 12$

9

10

11

12
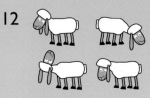

13

14

Think of things in your life that you count in 4s.

Copy and complete using doubling.

1. $3 \times 2 = 6$
   $3 \times 4 = 12$

1	$3 \times 2 = 6$		$3 \times 4 = \boxed{}$
2	$5 \times 2 = 10$		$5 \times 4 = \boxed{}$
3	$7 \times 2 = \boxed{}$		$7 \times 4 = \boxed{}$
4	$4 \times 2 = \boxed{}$		$4 \times 4 = \boxed{}$
5	$9 \times 2 = \boxed{}$		$9 \times 4 = \boxed{}$
6	$6 \times 2 = \boxed{}$		$6 \times 4 = \boxed{}$
7	$8 \times 2 = \boxed{}$		$8 \times 4 = \boxed{}$

Make the 8 times table using the 4 times table.

Each chair has four legs.
Write the number of legs.

8. $5 \times 4 = 20$

 8

9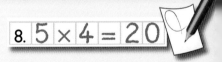

10	$2 \times 4 =$	11	$3 \times 4 =$	12	$10 \times 4 =$
13	$7 \times 4 =$	14	$4 \times 4 =$	15	$9 \times 4 =$
16	$6 \times 4 =$	17	$5 \times 4 =$	18	$8 \times 4 =$

Fours

Write the position of each pointer on the stick.

1. | 1 | 6 |

1
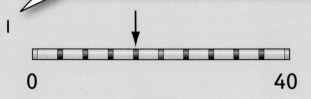
0   40

2
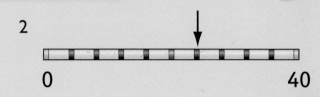
0   40

Copy and complete.

3. | 1 | 2 | ÷ | 4 | = | 3 |

3 12 ÷ 4 =

4 20 ÷ 4 =

5 40 ÷ 4 =

6 4 ÷ 4 =

7 36 ÷ 4 =

8 28 ÷ 4 =

9 32 ÷ 4 =

10 24 ÷ 4 =

11 16 ÷ 4 =

 Which numbers between 40 and 80 can be divided by 4?

12 How many season changes are there in 6 years?

 **13** Gary eats 4 slices of bread every day. How many slices does he eat in a fortnight?

14 The café has 4 chairs to each table. A coach party of 34 people come for a drink. How many tables will they need?

25

Fours

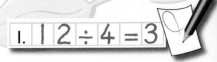

Copy and complete.

1. $12 \div$ $= 3$

2. $\times 4 = 20$

3. $\div 4 = 10$

4. $\times 4 = 28$

5. $\div 4 = 8$

6. $4 \div$ $= 1$

7. $\times 4 = 24$

8. $\times 4 = 36$

9. $\div 4 = 7$

True or false?

10. To multiply by 4, first multiply by 2, then double it.

11. Dividing a number by 4 is the same as finding one quarter of the number.

12. A multiple of 4 is always an even number.

Write the position of the pointer.

13.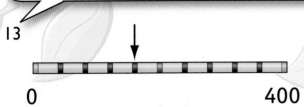

0   400

14.

0   400

Copy and complete.

15. $3 \times 40 =$

16. $5 \times 40 =$

17. $9 \times 40 =$

18. $6 \times 40 =$

19. $8 \times 40 =$

20. $7 \times 40 =$

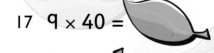

Turning

For each turn, write 'less than', 'more than' or 'equal to' a right angle.

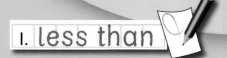
1. less than

1

2

3

4

5

6

How many right angles does the majorette turn her baton through?

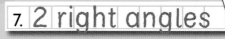
7. 2 right angles

7

8

9

10

11

12

For each baton above, draw the position when it has turned through another 5 right angles. What number of right-angle turns could end up in the same position?

Turning

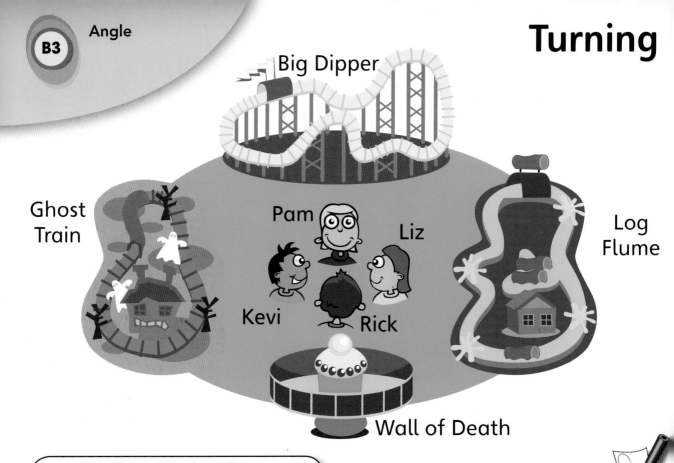

Big Dipper

Ghost Train

Pam Liz

Kevi Rick

Log Flume

Wall of Death

Write the ride that each child will face after these turns:

1. Ghost Train

Rick:
1 clockwise, 3 right angles
2 anticlockwise, 2 right angles

Liz:
3 anticlockwise, 1 right angle
4 clockwise, 3 right angles

Kevi:
5 clockwise, 2 right angles
6 anticlockwise, 1 right angle

Pam:
7 anticlockwise, 4 right angles
8 clockwise, 5 right angles

Rick's first turn leaves him facing the Ghost Train. How else could he have turned to face the same way? Repeat for the other children's turns too.

Design your own theme park! Write instructions like those above and ask your friend to answer the questions.

Turning

What number does the minute hand point to after these turns?

1

clockwise
1 right angle

2

anticlockwise
2 right angles

3

clockwise
3 right angles

4

clockwise
2 right angles

5

anticlockwise
1 right angle

6

clockwise
2 right angles

 I start at 11. One right-angle turn takes me to 2.
How else could I have got there? Describe the turns.

True or false?

7 If you turn clockwise through 1 right angle you face the same direction as turning anticlockwise through 3 right angles.

8 If you make a three-quarter turn clockwise, you face the same direction as turning anticlockwise through 2 right angles.

9 If you turn anticlockwise through 5 right angles you face the same direction as turning anticlockwise through 1 right angle.

10 In 5 minutes the minute hand of a clock turns through one-third of a right angle.

Turning

Use a clockface. Describe, in right angles, these clockwise turns of the minute hand.

A clockface showing the hands pointing to 8 and 6.

1
From: half past 7
To: 8 o'clock

2
From: quarter to 1
To: half past 1

3
From: ten past 3
To: twenty-five past 3

4
From: five past 6
To: ten to 7

5
From: five to 4
To: 4 o'clock

6
From: twenty-five to 10
To: five past 10

7
From: 5 o'clock
To: twenty past 5

8
From: 8 o'clock
To: ten to 9

Write your own 'from' and 'to' for the minute hand to turn through:

9 3 right angles

10 $\frac{2}{3}$ right angle

11 $1\frac{1}{3}$ right angles

12 $3\frac{2}{3}$ right angles

Describe some before and after times where the hour hand moves through 1 right angle.

North, South, East, West

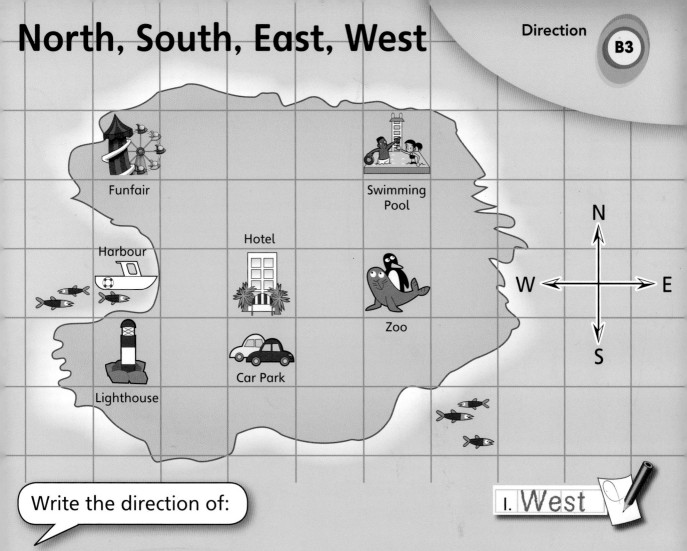

Write the direction of:

1. West

1 Harbour from Hotel

2 Zoo from Hotel

3 Lighthouse from Harbour

4 Pool from Funfair

5 Car Park from Hotel

6 Hotel from Car Park

7 Harbour from Zoo

8 Zoo from Swimming Pool

Look again at question I. You need to walk back to the hotel from the harbour. Which direction do you go in? Repeat this for the other questions.

Draw your own island on squared paper. Choose two places, then ask your friend to write the direction from one to the other.

North, South, East, West

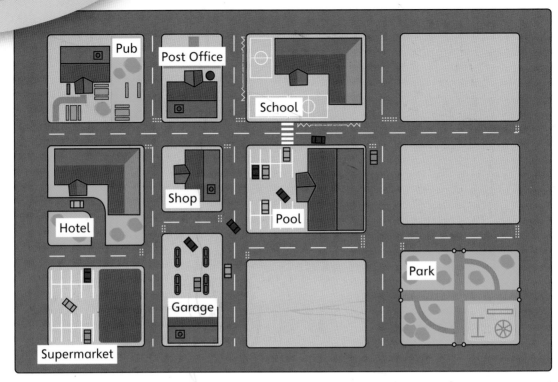

N

Write the direction of:

1. East

The Shop to: 1 Pool 2 Garage 3 Hotel

The Post Office to: 4 Pub 5 School 6 Garage

The Garage to: 7 Park 8 Post Office 9 Supermarket

Describe two directions to go from:

10. East, South

10 Pub to Shop via Post Office 11 Garage to Hotel via Supermarket

Describe a journey to visit all the places on the map.

North, South, East, West

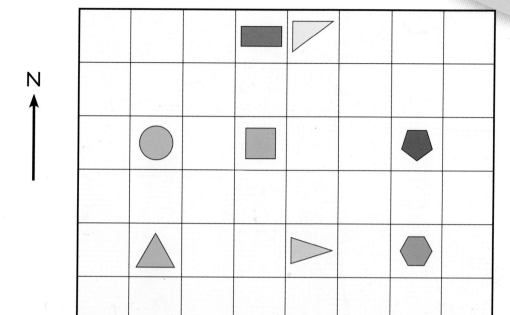

Draw the shape which is:

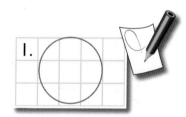

1. North of   2. South of   3. East of

4. West of   5. South of   6. East of

7. West of   8. North of   9. East of

10 South of , then East   11 North of , then West

12 South of , then West   13 East of , then North

Put two counters of different colours on the grid. Describe the position of one from the other to your friend. Then your friend describes the reverse.

North, South, East, West

1. East 2 km, North 2 km...

Describe each path.

1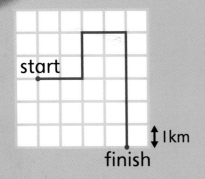

start

finish

↕ 1 km

2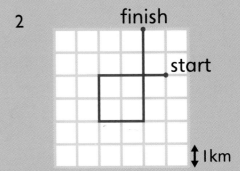

finish

start

↕ 1 km

3

start

finish

↕ 1 km

4

start

finish

↕ 1 km

 Draw your own paths on squared paper, and describe them.

Write the direction you face after these turns.

5 Face North, turn clockwise through 2 right angles

6 Face West, turn anticlockwise through 3 right angles

7 Face South, turn clockwise through 1 right angle

8 Face East, turn anticlockwise through 2 right angles

9 Face West, turn clockwise through 3 right angles

10 Face North, turn clockwise through 4 right angles

Grams

Write the weight of each object.

1. 600 grams

1

2

3

4

5

6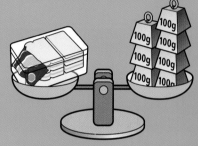

 My satchel can't weigh more than 1 kg. What objects can I put in it?

Read the scales. Write the weight.

7. 1 kg 300 g

7

8

9

10

11

12

13

14

15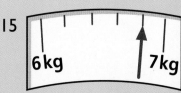

Grams and kilograms

Write each weight in grams.

1.  1100 g

 1 **1 kg 100 g**

2 **2 kg 600 g**

3 **3 kg 400 g**

4 **1½ kg**

5 **2 kg 300 g**

6 **4½ kg**

Write the weight of each sack in kilograms and grams.

7. **1 kg 200 g**

7 **1200 g**

8 **3½ kg**

9 **1700 g**

10 **1½ kg**

 If a tomato weighs 50 g, how many tomatoes will balance each sack?

Write how many of each will weigh 1 kilogram.

11. **10**

11 **100 g**

12 **500 g**

13 **200 g**

14 **50 g**

15 **10 g**

16

Grams and kilograms

1 A plum weighs 50 g. If I buy 1 kg of plums, how many plums will I have?

2 Each melon weighs 500 grams. What is the weight in kilograms of 10 melons?

3 Sarita bought a 5 kg bag of potatoes. A portion of potatoes weighs 400 g. What weight of potatoes is left after 10 portions have been eaten?

4 The contents of a tin of tomatoes weigh 100 g. A recipe requires 2 kg of tomatoes. How many tins are needed?

True or false?

5 Ten 100 g weights weigh 1 kilogram.

6 Two and a half kilograms is heavier than six 500 gram weights.

7 If tomatoes weigh 40 grams, a kilogram of tomatoes contains 22 tomatoes.

8 I kilogram of potatoes is heavier than 1 kilogram of feathers.

$\frac{1}{2}$ kg = 500 grams

9 Investigate other fractions of kilograms.

Position

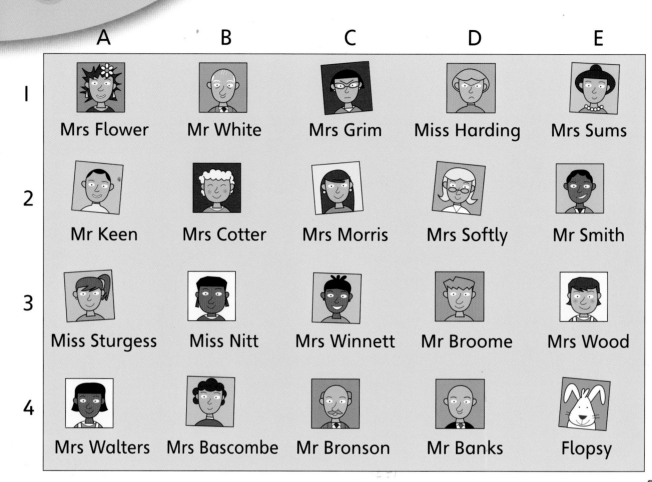

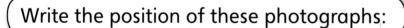

Write the position of these photographs:

I. C2

1 Mrs Morris	2 Mr Banks	3 Mr Smith
4 Miss Harding	5 Mr White	6 Mrs Walters
7 Mrs Softly	8 Mr Broome	9 Mrs Flower

Whose photographs are at these positions?

10 E1   11 A2   12 C3   13 E4   14 B2   15 C1

Look at a photograph. Tell your friend the position. Can they tell you who it is? Take turns at guessing.

Position

Describe the position of these animals:

1 chickens   2 hedgehogs   3 badgers   4 ducks

5 otters   6 horses   7 sheep   8 cows

What do the pictures at these positions show?

9 A1   10 A3   11 D2   12 E5   13 E2   14 D3

15 Which animals are in column D?

16 What do the pictures in row 2 show?

Draw your own grid of a garden.

Position

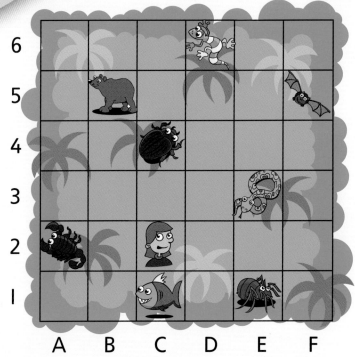

1 Tell Anna where the scary creatures are! Give the position of:

1. (a) E 3

a python   b bear   c spider   d bat

e scorpion   f piranha   g beetle   h lizard

Copy the grid. Make a letter of the alphabet by shading these positions.

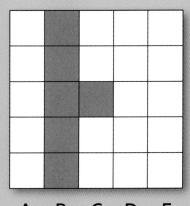

2 B1, B2, B3, B4, B5, C3, D1, D2, D3, D4, D5

3 A1, A2, A3, A4, A5, B3, B5, C5, B1, C1

4 B1, B2, B3, B4, C4, C1, D1, D2, D3, D4

Make a letter of your own on the grid. Describe the grid positions to your friend so that they can draw it. Take turns drawing and giving positions.

Months of the year

Write the months of the year in order, starting with January.

1

Spring

May   July
March   June
April   August

Summer

February   November
December   September
January   October

Winter   Autumn

Write the:

2 third month of the year

3 month after August

4 month before December

5 month between March and May

6 months with four letters or fewer

7 month between July and September

8 sixth month

9 months with an 'r' in

10 ninth month

11 month after January

My birthday month is in the summer and has four letters. Can you guess the month? Write a clue about your birthday month for your friend to answer.

Days and weeks

Write how many days old.

1. 15 days

1
2 weeks
1 day

2
3 weeks
3 days

3
1 week
5 days

4
5 weeks
1 day

5
4 weeks
6 days

6
7 weeks
1 day

7
3 weeks
2 days

8
3 weeks
1 day

Write in weeks and days.

9. 2 weeks 3 days

9

17 days to Christmas

10

20 days to Diwali

11

50 days to holiday

12

25 days to party

13

30 days to
my birthday

14

100 days to
Chinese New Year

Find out how long it is to the end of
term, and to the start of next term.

Days, weeks, months and years

Time **C3**

Write how old each elephant is in years and months.

1. I year I month

1 13 months

3 26 months

2 18 months

4 39 months

5 50 months

6 120 months

Write the number of:

7	days in a week	8	months in a year
9	weeks in a year	10	months in 2 years
11	days in a year	12	years in a century

Write the number of months in a millennium. Can you work out the number of weeks?

13 At the end of term, Greg had a 4-week holiday. He went abroad for 18 days, then went camping for 9 days. How many holiday days are left?

14 There are 30 days in April. Jim's birthday was on 23rd April. What is the date 3 weeks after his birthday?

Calendars

July						
Monday	Tuesday	Wednesday	Thursday	Friday	Saturday	Sunday
	1	2	3	4	5	6
7	8	9	10	11	12	13
14	15	16	17	18	19	20
21	22	23	24	25	26	27
28	29	30	31			

What day of the week are these dates?

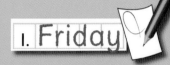
1. Friday

1 4th   2 10th   3 22nd   4 6th   5 19th

6 12th   7 31st   8 25th   9 15th   10 29th

What is the date in July of:

11 the second Friday   12 the third Tuesday

13 the fourth Sunday   14 the first Saturday

15 the last Wednesday   16 one week after the 17th

17 one week after the 4th   18 one week before the 12th

19 **Investigate different numbers of days.**

Try these:
- the number of days we have had this year
- the number of days to go until the end of the year
- the number of days you have lived.

Think of some more days you could investigate.

Venn diagrams

Copy the Venn diagram. Make sure you draw it big enough! Write each name in the correct place.

Gita   Chuy

Amit   Tom

Raj   May

Bella   Debbie

Zoe   Paul

Ann   John

Mick   Natalie

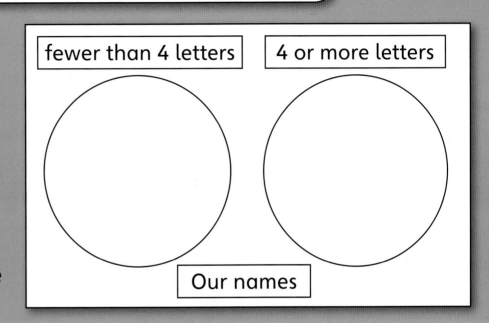

fewer than 4 letters   4 or more letters

Our names

Copy the Venn diagram. Think of more words to write on it.

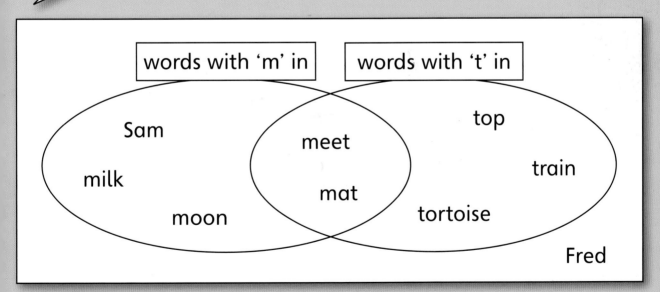

words with 'm' in   words with 't' in

Sam

milk

moon

meet

mat

top

train

tortoise

Fred

Draw a Venn diagram to show something about your toys, for example 'with wheels' or 'no wheels'.

Carroll diagrams

Look at the Carroll diagram. Write the words that should go in each section.

	Joining word	Not joining word
Short word (fewer than 4 letters)		
Long word (4 or more letters)		

cat

where

but

table

dog

chair

and

which

because

Use a book to find and write more words on the diagram.

What could the column and row headings be on this Carroll diagram?

	remote-control car	doll teddy
	TV computer	bike pogo stick

Carroll and Venn diagrams

Copy the Carroll diagram. Write the words that should go in each section. Think of other words to write on the diagram.

	2 syllables or fewer	More than 2 syllables
Words rhyming with sea		
Words not rhyming with sea		

summery

autumn

tree

wasp

wispy

beautiful

blustery

cheerfully

spring

imagining

wind

bee

free

sun

Transfer all this information onto a Venn diagram. What labels will the two sets have?

Choose 20 words from a book. Guess which boxes on the page will have more words. Sort the words. Was your guess correct?

Carroll and Venn diagrams

Look at the Venn diagram. Draw a Carroll diagram to sort into the same categories. Add another 10 animals to the diagram.

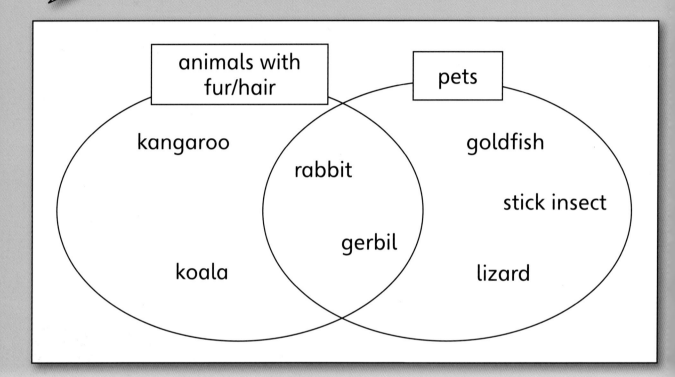

Sort numbers between 20 and 50 onto this diagram.

	Multiples of 3	Not multiples of 3
Odd		
Even		

Change the number of the multiples so that there will not be any number in one of the regions.

Adding

How old will each parrot be?

1. $30 + 20 = 50$
   $6 + 3 = 9$
   $50 + 9 = 59$

1

36 years

lives 23
more years

2

54 years

lives 24
more years

3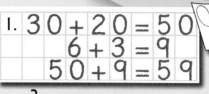

67 years

lives 21
more years

4

72 years

lives 27
more years

5

53 years

lives 44
more years

6

65 years

lives 25
more years

Complete these additions.

7. $40 + 30 = 70$
   $8 + 6 = 14$
   $70 + 14 = 84$

7 48 + 36

8 65 + 37

9 56 + 36

10 39 + 44

11 57 + 26

12 42 + 38

13 Jim has £54. His brother has saved £38. They want to buy a bike for £100. How much more must they save?

Find pairs of numbers that add to 100 where all four digits are different.

Adding

Write the total length of the ribbons.

```
1. 36 + 47 + 54
   30 + 40 + 50 = 120
         6 + 7 + 4 = 17
     120 + 17 = 137 cm
```

1

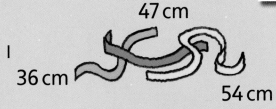

47 cm

36 cm

54 cm

2

28 cm

42 cm

38 cm

3

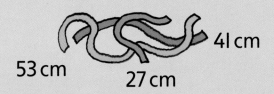

53 cm

27 cm

41 cm

4

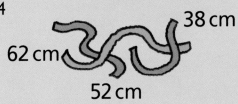

62 cm

52 cm

38 cm

Estimate the total length of all the ribbons by rounding each answer to the nearest 10 cm and adding. How close is your total to the actual length?

5 Amit bought a coat for £36, trousers for £24 and jeans for £48. How much did he spend?

6 Molly saved £45. She sold her bike for £58. She earned £36 washing cars. How much did she have?

Copy and complete.

```
7. 146 + 32 + 64
    40 + 30 + 60 = 130
         6 + 2 + 4 = 12
   100 + 130 + 12 = 242
```

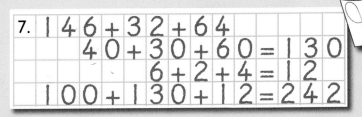

7 146 + 32 + 64

8 128 + 37 + 56

9 135 + 28 + 36

10 245 + 27 + 26

11 117 + 36 + 45

12 241 + 27 + 18

Adding

Write the total weight of sweets.

1. $100 + 80 + 17 = 197g$

1 116 g 47 g 34 g

2 128 g 36 g 37 g

3 35 g 145 g 47 g

4 42 g 58 g 137 g

5 44 g 33 g 155 g

6 78 g 55 g 124 g

7 Can you help me? I have these cards:

| 1 | 2 | 3 | 4 | 5 | 6 | 7 |

What is the largest total that can be made from an addition like this:

H T U   T U   T U

☐☐☐ + ☐☐ + ☐☐

What if the card 1 is replaced by 0 ?

Copy and complete.

8 £146 + £58 + £37 =

9 £128 + £64 + £32 =

10 £117 + £86 + £18 =

11 £127 + £54 + £31 =

Each donkey is carrying a rider and two saddlebags. How much weight in total?

I. $100+100=200$
$20+50+10=80$
$7+4+5=16$
$200+80+16=296\,kg$

1 Rider: 127 kg
   Bag 1: 54 kg
   Bag 2: 115 kg

2 Rider: 124 kg
   Bag 1: 110 kg
   Bag 2: 36 kg

3 Rider: 112 kg
   Bag 1: 73 kg
   Bag 2: 23 kg

4 Rider: 105 kg
   Bag 1: 57 kg
   Bag 2: 85 kg

 Using these cards: 1 2 3 4 5 6 7 8 9

in order, what is the answer to this addition?

Try in reverse order.

November						
Mon	Tue	Wed	Thu	Fri	Sat	Sun
1	2	3	4	5	6	7
8	9	10	11	12	13	14
15	16	17	18	19	20	21
22	23	24	25	26	27	28
29	30					

5 Addy drives 128 miles to see his mum. He then drives 26 miles to the beach, and 147 miles home. How far has he driven?

6 It is 128 days until Christmas. Then it is 46 days until Lucy's birthday. Then it is 54 days until her big holiday! How long to wait?

 Add some 3-digit numbers to make exactly 1000. Can you do this in several different ways?

Adding

Copy and complete.

	T U		T U		T U		T U
1	3 6	2	3 6	3	2 8	4	4 5
	+ 2 3		+ 4 2		+ 9 1		+ 3 4
	5 9		*7 8*		*1 1 9*		*7 9*

	T U		T U		T U		T U
5	1 7	6	3 2	7	5 1	8	4 2
	+ 4 2		+ 1 2		+ 2 5		+ 3 3
	5 9		*4 4*		*7 6*		*7 5*

1.
```
   6 0
    T U
    3 6
  + 2 3
      9
    5 0
    5 9
```

Choose two items. Add them. Write the total.

£39

£48 ✓

£18

£27 ✓

£25

£ (obscured)

£53 ✓

£49 ✓

£28

9.
```
 £ 7 0
    T U
  + 2 7
    3 9
  £ 6 6
      1
```

Find two numbers which can be added to give
51. Both numbers must have a units digit greater
than or equal to 5.   5   5

53 + 48 = £101

Adding

Copy and complete.

1	T U
	4 6
	2 8
	+ 7 3
	———

2	T U
	6 8
	3 7
	+ 4 5
	———

3	T U
	7 3
	8 1
	+ 2 4
	———

4	T U
	3 8
	1 4
	+ 3 2
	———

5	T U
	5 6
	2 7
	+ 3 9
	———

6	T U
	4 8
	3 3
	+ 1 7
	———

7	T U
	6 2
	3 7
	+ 2 6
	———

1.
```
  1 5 0
  H T U
    4 6
    2 8
  + 7 3
  -----
    1 7
  1 3 0
  -----
  1 4 7
```

8 Choose a fuel pod, then add it to a rocket. How long in total? Do this 4 times.

8.
```
  2 0 0 m
  H T U
  + 1 5 6
    5 4
  -----
  2 1 0 m
    1 1
```

68 m

168 m

37 m

54 m

156 m

36 m

135 m

137 m

43 m

Two rockets have a total length of 400 m. What could the fuel pod and rocket lengths be?

Adding

Copy and complete.

1.
```
    H T U
    2 9 0
    2 4 7
  +   3 8
    2 8 5
        1
```

```
1   H T U
    2 4 7
  +   3 8
  _____
```

```
2   H T U
    1 6 4
  +   5 8
  _____
```

```
3   H T U
    3 8 2
  +   6 4
  _____
```

```
4   H T U
    1 3 8
  +   1 6
  _____
```

```
5   H T U
    1 4 6
  +   3 7
  _____
```

```
6   H T U
    1 2 8
  +   3 1
  _____
    1 8 3
```

```
7   H T U
    4 6 3
  +   6 9
  _____
```

8 Ray has collected 365 stamps. His uncle sends him 46 new ones from Africa. His aunt sends him 26 from India. How many does he have now?

9 Boston Bank has 564 thousand pounds in its vault. The bank manager deposits another 58 thousand pounds. How many thousands now?

10 It is 184 miles from Exeter to London. It is 56 miles further to the Channel Tunnel. How far from Exeter to the Channel Tunnel?

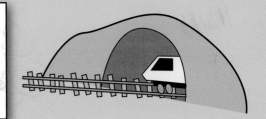

Invent your own word problem involving adding two numbers with an answer of 999.

Copy and complete.

I.

	H	T	U
	6	4	0
	3	7	4
+	2	6	8
	6	4	2
		1	1

1

	H	T	U
	3	7	4
+	2	6	8

2

	H	T	U
	2	8	6
+	4	1	8

3

	H	T	U
	3	7	5
+	1	8	8

4

	H	T	U
	2	7	8
+	1	8	7

5

	H	T	U
	3	9	2
+	1	2	9

6

	H	T	U
	1	8	8
+	2	7	6

7

	H	T	U
	2	8	3
+	3	7	9

8

```
  C A T
+ D O G
-------
  R O W
```

Each letter represents a digit. No digit is represented by more than one letter. Write the sum in numbers. Hint: O = I. Use number cards to help.

Both these people received their telegram from the Queen. They were over 100 when they died! Write the year they died.

9 Granny Eliza was born in 1900 and got married aged 28. Then she was a village shopkeeper for 46 years. She was retired for 27 years.

10 Grandpa Will was born in 1898 and got married aged 28. After that he was a postman for 45 years, and then lived in retirement for 28 years.

Difference

Count on to find the difference.

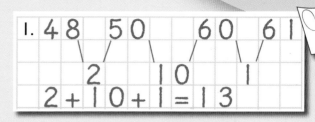

1. 48 50   60 61
      2   10   1
   2 + 10 + 1 = 13

1 48 → 61   2 27 → 52   3 38 → 75

4 45 → 62   5 66 → 83   6 54 → 71

Find the difference between the purses.

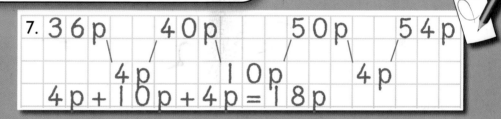

7. 36p   40p   50p   54p
       4p   10p   4p
   4p + 10p + 4p = 18p

7 36p 54p

8 42p 35p

9  61p 57p

10 45p 63p

11 68p 82p

12 53p 78p

13 Toni has 65p and Amy has 82p. How much must Toni save to have the same as Amy?

14 Fred is 37 years old and his sister Sophie is 18. How many years' difference in their ages?

Write your own story involving finding a difference.

Difference

Count on to find the difference.

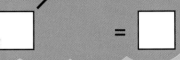

1. $3 + 10 + 5 = 18$

1   605 – 587

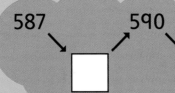

587 → ☐ → 590 → ☐ → 600 → ☐ → 605 = ☐

2   312 – 274   3   405 – 364   4   510 – 471   5   208 – 157

Find the difference between the tree heights.

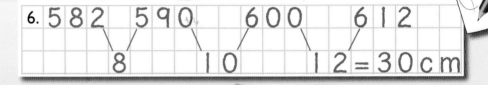

6. 582 → 590 → 600 → 612
        8   10   12 = 30 cm

6

582 cm   612 cm

7

767 cm   802 cm

8

311 cm   278 cm

9

456 cm   539 cm

10
268 cm   377 cm

11

553 cm   619 cm

12

321 cm   488 cm

13

832 cm   754 cm

The difference in height between two trees is 30 cm.
One is taller than 5 m and one is shorter than 5 m.
What could the total of their two heights be?

Difference

Find the difference between the two prices.

1. $2 + 30 + 16 = 48$
difference = £48

1   £516   £468

£516

468 → □ → 470 → □ → 500 → □ → 516 = □

£468

2   £402   £388   3   £354   £408   4   £383   £418

 The total cost of two bikes is £1000. There is a £50 difference in price between them. How much does each one cost?

5   Molly's walk to school is 752 m. If she goes to pick up her friend Mandy on the way, her walk is 814 m. How much longer is it to pick up Mandy?

6   Ling climbs a tor on Dartmoor. At the top, she has climbed 652 m. Her brother only gets to 587 m. How much further did Ling climb?

Write the change from £5.

7. $3p + 30p = 33p$

7   8   9   10   11

 £4·67

£3·66

 £2·81

 £4·58

 £2·87

Find the difference between the two scores by counting on.

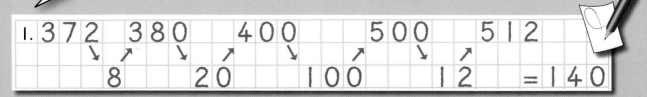

1. 372 380 400 500 512
8 20 100 12 = 140

1
372
512

2
464
621

3
713
575

4
562
711

5
326
542

6
265
432

I use next-door digits to make a 3-digit number. The first and last digits are the same, for example 656.

I swap the digits to make another 3-digit number, for example 565.

Find the difference between the two. Do this six times. What do you notice?

Find the following:

7   the difference between 482 and 531

8   38 less than 517

9   76 more than 283

10   the total of 145 and 58

11   two numbers with a difference of 32

12   47 less than 423

Subtraction

Copy and complete.

1.
$$64 = 60 + 4$$
$$-30 \quad -30$$
$$\overline{} \quad 30 + 4 = 34$$

1	64 – 30	2	78 – 22	3	86 – 12
4	76 – 20	5	69 – 34	6	88 – 40

Each painter moves down one rung (22 cm). Write the new height.

7.
$$84 = 80 + 4$$
$$-22 \quad -20 + 2$$
$$\overline{} \quad 60 + 2 = 62\ cm$$

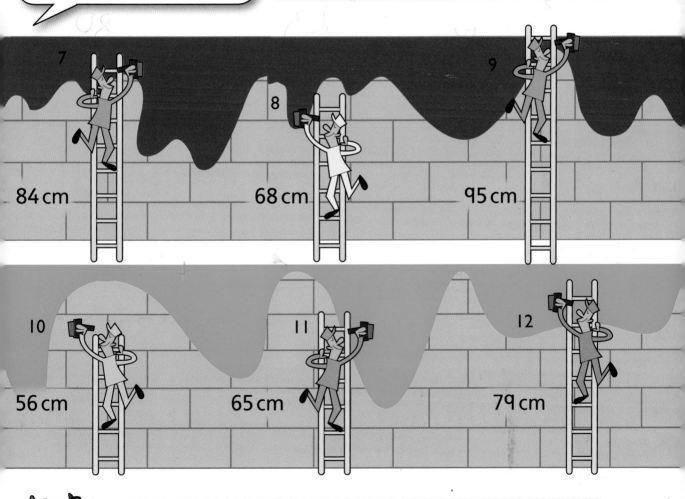

7   84 cm

8   68 cm

9   95 cm

10   56 cm

11   65 cm

12   79 cm

What if the painter came down two rungs at a time? Write the new height. Explore for three rungs.

Subtraction

55

Write the new length of the log.

1.
```
 88 =  80 + 8
-23   -20 + 3
       60 + 5 = 65 cm
```

1
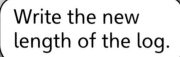
65
88 cm
23 cm chopped

2
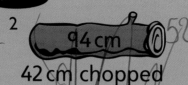
52
94 cm
42 cm chopped
90 - 4 = 86

3
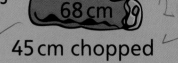
23
68 cm
45 cm chopped

4
78 cm
32 cm chopped
46

5
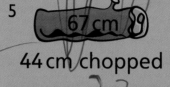
67 cm
44 cm chopped
23

6
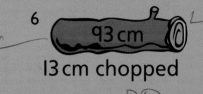
93 cm
13 cm chopped
80

A log is 64 cm long. Each day one quarter of its new length is chopped off. After how many days will it be less than 20 cm long?

Write the new thread length.

7.
```
 43 =  40 + 3 =  30 + 13
-28   -20 + 8   -20 +  8
                 10 +  5 = 15 cm
```

7
43 cm
rises 28 cm
15

8
68 cm
rises 31 cm

9 9 - 4 = 5 so 55 - 2 = 53
95 cm
rises 42 cm
53

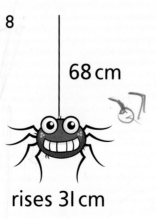

10
28 cm
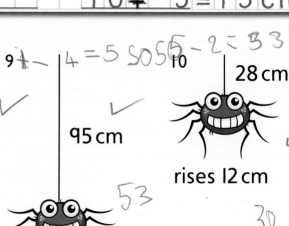
rises 12 cm
30

43 - 28
40 - 20 = 20 - 3 = 17

Subtraction

How much has each child got left?

1.	54 =	50 + 4 =	40 + 14
	− 3 7	− 3 0 + 7	− 3 0 + 7
			10 + 7 = 17 p

1  54p 17p ✓
spends 37p

2  68p ✓ 19p
spends 49p

3  43p 16p ✓
spends 27p

4  72p 34 ✓
spends 38p

5  54p 28 p ✓
spends 26p

6 65p ✓✓
spends 17p 48 p

= 34. 44 82

7 Choose two snakes. Find the difference in their lengths.

7.	82 =	80 + 2 =	70 + 12
	− 6 6	− 6 0 + 6	− 6 0 + 6
			10 + 6 = 16 cm

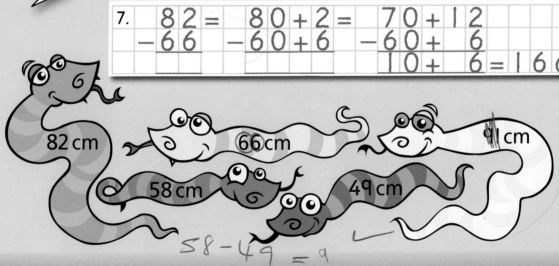

82 cm   66 cm   1 cm
58 cm   49 cm

58 − 49 = 9 ✓

8 Sam is 45 years old. Her mum is 71 years old. How old was her mum when Sam was born?

Sam = 45
Mum 71

7 11
45. 2 6

9 Cal has £33. Wayne has £61. How much more has Wayne got?

7 − 4 = 30 + 5 = 35

Subtraction

Write the new height.

1.
```
 362 =  300 + 60 + 2 =  300 + 50 + 12
-  48 -              40 + 8 -          40 +  8
                                 300 + 10 +  4 = 314 m
```

1   362 m   falls 48 m

2   453 m   falls 39 m

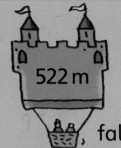

3   522 m   falls 18 m

4   384 m   falls 67 m

5   452 m   falls 29 m

6   493 m   falls 56 m

Check the subtractions. Correct the wrong ones!

7.
```
 468 =  400 + 60 + 8 =  400 + 50 + 18
-  19 -             10 + 9 -         10 +  9
                                400 + 40 +  9 = 44
```

7   $468 - 19 = 449$ 8 $544 - 29 = 525$ 9 $372 - 38 = 304$

10   $494 - 68 = 426$ 11 $567 - 29 = 528$ 12 $482 - 37 = 445$

Invent three subtractions for your friend, one of which is wrong.

Dividing

Write a division to match each set of cubes.

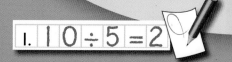

1. $10 \div 5 = 2$

1
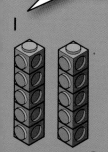

2
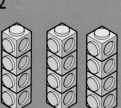

3
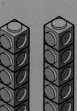

4

$2 \div 10 = 5$

5

6

7

8
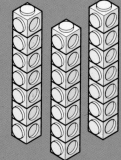

Write a matching multiplication for each division.

Draw strips of squares to show these divisions.

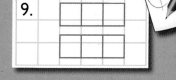

9.

9   $6 \div 3$ 10 $30 \div 5$ 11 $14 \div 2$

12 $16 \div 4$ 13 $18 \div 6$ 14 $21 \div 3$

15

There are 8 packets of 4 stickers.
Your mum gives you 3 a day. How many days will it take to get all the stickers?

Dividing with remainders

Complete these divisions with remainders. Use the multiplication grid to help you.

1. $11 \div 3 = 3 \, r \, 2$

1   $11 \div 3 =$ 2 $17 \div 2 =$

3   $24 \div 5 =$ 4 $31 \div 4 =$

5   $19 \div 3 =$ 6 $34 \div 6 =$

7   $9 \div 2 =$ 8 $18 \div 5 =$

9   $22 \div 4 =$ 10 $40 \div 6 =$

11 $52 \div 5 =$ 12 $34 \div 3 =$

1	2	3	4	5	6	7	8	9	10
2	4	6	8	10	12	14	16	18	
3	6	9	12	15	18	21			
4	8	12	16	20	24				
5	10	15	20	25	30				

How many numbers, up to 60, can be divided by exactly 2, 3, 4, 5 or 6?

13   A box of 16 eggs is used to make omelettes, each using 3 eggs. How many omelettes can be made, and how many eggs are left over?

14   Kylie had 35p and bought as many 4p sweets as she could. How many coins could she have left?

Here is a story for $17 \div 7 = 2 \, r \, 3$:

It is 17 days before my birthday. That is 2 whole weeks and 3 days left over.

Write a story for:

15   $11 \div 2 = 5 \, r \, 1$

16   $15 \div 4 = 3 \, r \, 3$

Dividing with remainders

The Furry Animals are having a football competition. They call it the FA Cup. The 32 animals are to be put into teams. Write how many teams, and how many left-over animals.

1. $32 \div 3 = 10 \, r \, 2$

1	teams of 3	2	teams of 4
3	teams of 5	4	teams of 6
5	teams of 7	6	teams of 8
7	teams of 9	8	teams of 10
9	teams of 11		

I'm making teams of 4. How many players must there be so that one can be the referee?

10 Use these number cards:

0 1 2 3 4 5 6 7 8 9 ÷ = r

Use the cards to create a division with a remainder:

1 5 ÷ 6 = 2 r 3

Make 10 different divisions. Can you think of any more?

Dividing with remainders

Copy and complete.

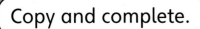

1. $28 \div 3 = 9 \text{ r } 1$

1   $28 \div 3 =$

2   $45 \div 7 =$

3   $39 \div 4 =$

4   $27 \div 5 =$

5   $19 \div 2 =$

6   $43 \div 8 =$

7   $29 \div 9 =$

8   $19 \div 6 =$

9   $73 \div 10 =$

True or false?

10   If an odd number is divided by an even number, there is always a remainder.

11   If an even number is divided by an odd number, there is always a remainder.

12   Multiples of 6 have no remainder when divided by 3.

13   Multiples of 3 have no remainder when divided by 6.

14   If a number has a remainder when divided by 5, it will also have a remainder when divided by 10.

15   When 23 is divided by 4 the remainder is greater than when 29 is divided by 5.

Can you give reasons for your answers?

Multiplying by 10 and 100

These centipedes have 100 legs. How many legs in each set?

1. $3 \times 100 = 300$

1

2

3

4

5

6

These centipedes can run 10 centimetres in 1 minute. How far can they run in:

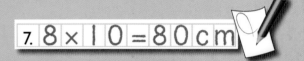

7. $8 \times 10 = 80 \text{ cm}$

7   8 minutes

8   3 minutes

9   6 minutes

10 11 minutes

11 120 seconds

12 300 seconds

How many metres will a centipede run in 1 hour?

Copy and complete.

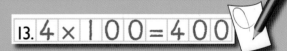

13. $4 \times 100 = 400$

13 $4 \times 100 =$

14 $7 \times 10 =$

15 $9 \times 100 =$

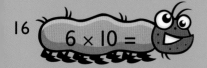
16 $6 \times 10 =$

17 $1 \times 100 =$

18 $2 \times 10 =$

Multiplying

The kangaroos hold a long jump competition.
Write how many centimetres each kangaroo jumps.

1. 3 × 100 = 300 cm

3 metres

2
7 metres

3
5 metres

9 metres

5
$4\frac{1}{2}$ metres

6
3 metres 21 centimetres

 How many more metres would it take for each kangaroo to reach 10 m?

Write how many beads.

7. 3 × 20 = 60

7
8
9
10
11
12

 I want to make necklaces using 10 beads of each colour. How many necklaces can I make, and how many beads will be left over?

Multiplying

Write the cost of the masks.

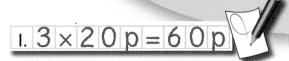

1. $3 \times 20p = 60p$

20p   40p   30p   50p

1 3 clown masks   2 2 teddy bear masks

3 5 alien masks   4 7 monkey masks

5 6 clown masks   6 4 teddy bear masks

7 3 alien masks   8 9 monkey masks

9 10 alien masks and 4 monkey masks

10 6 teddy bear masks and 5 clown masks

How many of each mask can you buy for £5?

Copy and complete.

11. $3 \times 30 = 90$

11  3×30

12 5×40

13  6×30

14 8×50

15 40×3

16  4×20

17 50×5

18 9×30

19  2×60

Multiplying

1 Kate bought 5 grapefruit for 30p each. How much change does she have from £2?

2 Matchboxes hold 50 matches. They are sold in packs of 5 boxes. How many matches in a pack? How many packs must I buy to have 1000 matchsticks?

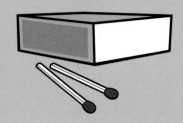

3 The circus seats are in rows of 40. If 140 people try to sit in the front 3 rows, how many will not be able to get a seat?

4 The Jolly Giant grows 20 cm every week. He is now 310 cm tall. How tall will he be in 4 weeks' time?

Copy and write the missing numbers.

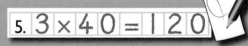
5. 3 × 40 = 120

5 3 × 40 = ☐

6 5 × 40 = ☐

7 4 × ☐ = 120

8 ☐ × 3 = 180

9 50 × ☐ = 150

10 ☐ × 4 = 240

11 80 × ☐ = 400

12 7 × 500 = ☐

13 9 × ☐ = 3600

Look at my multiplications! Find the numbers that fit. Can you find other pairs like these?

☐ × 30 = ☐ × 40

☐ × 50 = ☐ × 20

Fractions

Write the fraction of red buttons.

1. $\frac{1}{4}$

1 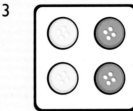 2 3 4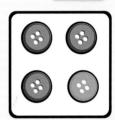

5 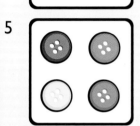 6 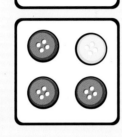 7 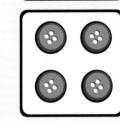 8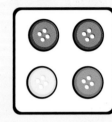

 Choose some other colours. Write the fractions.

Write the fraction of clowns that are:

9 happy

10 sad

11 looking left

12 looking right

13 wearing a bow tie

14 wearing a hat

15 happy and wearing a hat

16 sad and looking left

Fractions

Use each picture to write a pair of matching fractions.

1. $\frac{1}{2}$ and $\frac{2}{4}$

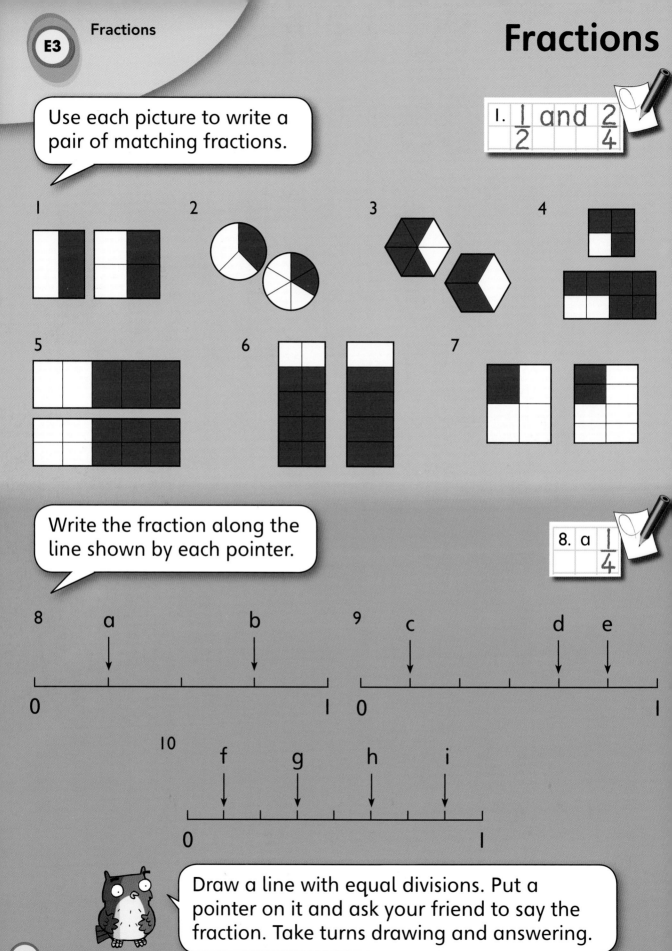

Write the fraction along the line shown by each pointer.

8. a $\frac{1}{4}$

Draw a line with equal divisions. Put a pointer on it and ask your friend to say the fraction. Take turns drawing and answering.

Fractions

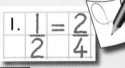

$\frac{1}{12}$	$\frac{1}{12}$	$\frac{1}{12}$	$\frac{1}{12}$	$\frac{1}{12}$	$\frac{1}{12}$	$\frac{1}{12}$	$\frac{1}{12}$	$\frac{1}{12}$	$\frac{1}{12}$	$\frac{1}{12}$	$\frac{1}{12}$
$\frac{1}{6}$		$\frac{1}{6}$		$\frac{1}{6}$		$\frac{1}{6}$		$\frac{1}{6}$		$\frac{1}{6}$	
$\frac{1}{4}$			$\frac{1}{4}$			$\frac{1}{4}$			$\frac{1}{4}$		
$\frac{1}{3}$				$\frac{1}{3}$				$\frac{1}{3}$			
$\frac{1}{2}$						$\frac{1}{2}$					
I whole											

Copy and write the missing numbers.

1. $\frac{1}{2} = \frac{2}{4}$

1 $\frac{1}{2} = \dfrac{\Box}{4}$

2 $\frac{1}{3} = \dfrac{\Box}{6}$

3 $\frac{2}{3} = \dfrac{\Box}{6}$

4 $\frac{6}{6} = \dfrac{\Box}{3}$

5 $\frac{1}{2} = \dfrac{3}{\Box}$

6 $\frac{3}{4} = \dfrac{\Box}{12}$

7 $\frac{3}{12} = \dfrac{1}{\Box}$

8 $\frac{4}{12} = \dfrac{1}{\Box}$

9 $\frac{8}{12} = \dfrac{\Box}{3}$

10 Annie cycles 5 km on a 10 km track.
Ben cycles 15 km along a track of 25 km.
Ben has done more of his track than
Annie has of her track – true or false?

11 Mena has to give away 3 out of 6 marbles.
Becky has to give away 4 out of her 8 marbles.
Are they giving away the same fraction?

Fractions

Write pairs of letters to match pairs of fractions.

1. a and ...

1

a $\frac{1}{2}$

b two-thirds

c $\frac{2}{5}$

d $\frac{6}{10}$

e one-third

f $\frac{1}{4}$

g $\frac{2}{3}$

h three-quarters

i $\frac{6}{8}$

j $\frac{2}{4}$

k three-ninths

l $\frac{4}{6}$

m $\frac{4}{10}$

n three-fifths

o $\frac{8}{12}$

p $\frac{3}{12}$

Use number cards 1 to 10.

2

| 1 | 2 | 3 | 4 | 5 | 6 | 7 | 8 | 9 | 10 |

Use four cards to make a pair of matching fractions. There are 17 in total – can you find them all?

$$\frac{2}{3} = \frac{4}{6}$$

Using £ and pence notation

> Write the amount in each purse.

1. £1·24

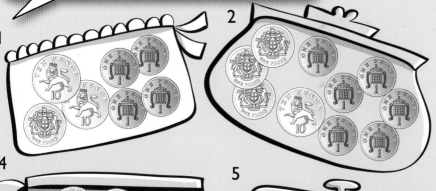

> Write the £1, 10p and 1p coins needed to make each amount.

7. 3 × £1
   4 × 10p
   2 × 1p

7   £3·42

8   £5·61

9   £2·21

10   £3·99

11   £9·30

12   £4·68

13   £2·19

14   £1·05

> True or false?

15 Any amount which is more than £1 can be made using a pound coin.

16 £1·11 can be made using three coins.

17 If you have four coins then £1·51 is the most you can make.

What amounts can be made using two coins, where one is £1? How about if one is £2?

Using £ and pence notation

Write each amount in pounds and pence.

1. £4·65

1 465p
2 184p
3 257p
4 880p
5 104p
6 777p
7 356p
8 605p
9 900p
10 1010p

James saves 1p each day of the year. How many days to save each amount?

11. 416 days

11 £4·16
12 £3·72
13 £2·81
14 £5·25
15 £3·18
16 £9·09
17 £10·78
18 £6·60

Which ones take less than a year? How about 2 years?

19 Simon has 4 coins. He has twice as many and double that number of . How much does he have?

20 Vicky saves 5p coins. She has collected 25. How much does she have?

If I have no £1 coins, what is the fewest number of coins I need to make £1.99?

Money problems

Choose three items. Add the prices. Write the total in £ and pence. Repeat six times.

```
  8 5
  4 4
  7 6
2 0 5 p
£ 2·0 5
```

85p

39p

13p

54p

76p

62p

95p

44p

28p

67p

Write the fewest coins needed to pay for each item.

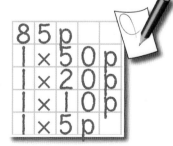

```
8 5 p
1 × 5 0 p
1 × 2 0 p
1 × 1 0 p
1 × 5 p
```

Jenny has four silver coins. What amounts could she have? What is the most? What is the least?

Money problems

Write how you would make each amount. Use the fewest coins possible!

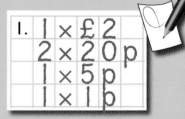

1.
| 1 × £2 |
| 2 × 20p |
| 1 × 5p |
| 1 × 1p |

| 1 | £2·46 | 2 | £1·19 | 3 | £1·86 | 4 | £2·59 | 5 | £3·11 |
| 6 | £5·53 | 7 | £4·25 | 8 | £3·33 | 9 | £5·09 | 10 | £1·90 |

How much would you have to add to each to get to the next pound?

1. £2·46 + 54p = £3

11 Rachel has one newly-minted coin of each type. How much does she have?

12 Gus has two £2 coins. He buys three tickets at 49p each. How much does he have left?

13 Afram has an amount of money that can be written forwards or backwards (like £3·63). He has £1 coins, 20p coins and 1p coins. He has more than £4 and less than £5. How much could he have?

14 Cathy has 10 coins: three 10p coins and some £1 coins and 1p coins. What amounts could she have?

I have 50 coins all of the same type. List the different amounts I could have.